ACKNOWLEDGEMENTS

For providing real-world inspiration for these poems, thank you to my parents, my sister Rachel, Jason Palmer, and the entire congregation of Calvary Temple (AKA Southgate Church) in my hometown of South Bend, Indiana. For reading and commenting on earlier drafts of this manuscript, thanks to Laura Mullen, Lara Glenum, Benjy Kahan, Vincent Cellucci, and the entire LSU MFA family. God knows I couldn't have done this without your ceaseless support and encouragement.

FIRST APPEARANCES

Thanks to all the hardworking staff at the following journals, in which many of these poems (or alternate versions) first appeared:

Birds of Lace's "30 x Lace" ("saint drain")

Crab Fat ("automessiah" & "sacred sucre")

Deluge ("original schism" & "Agateophobia"/"phobiaphile 6")

Foothill ("peri-" & "Acarophobia"/ "phobiaphile 5")

Gobbet ("X-machine," "the tundran," & "visit station")

Juked ("in media rape" & "bad news, new world order")

la fovea ("rite hype")

The Lost Piece ("filled")

Small Po[r]tions ("biblical umbilical")

So and So ("why's virus")

Smoking Glue Gun ("phobiaphile 1-3")

Tenderloin ("a ritual feeding // in need of meter," "swaddling plot," "canticle cannibal," "ménage à trinity," & "how a godhead cums // to earn his stripes")

For my family

and all god's
little trauma children

lonely kneeling
molested & infected

for they shall
inherit his girth

Dylan
Krieger

Giving
Godhead

But picture, in your own terms, the frightful God you preach: he has but one son; an only son, begot of some passing strange commerce; for, as man doth fuck, so he hath willed that his Lord fucketh too; and the Lord didst detach and send down out of Heaven this respectable part of himself.

Marquis de Sade
Philosophy in the Bedroom

I

Quid Pro Blow

in media rape

the dream starts *in media rape*—rate the me meat one to ten on
reddit—as in that meat is so you it's upsetting—a bottle of upchuck
containing my darling—bad doG! goes BLEEP when you gut her—
soft-eyed and swirled in linoleum butter—I swallow too hard at the
edge of the gutter—my dinosaur muzzle the size of a meadow—
remember? december—how red then—all the felled leaves fraught
in HD and glued to a soundstage—forever as glitter—the ball turret
gunner spun out of its socket—I wanted a pixel to picture his
nothing—a wristwatch, a kerchief, a lisp from his mother—but the
wonder is the wokeup—the wonder is I choke up—an avalanche of
first-world excess—first thing every morning—when the curser
points too far down—my holy hologram—esophagus and—clicks

rectifire

look mom: safety first
I'm performing this
sexorcism via skype
like *lick my creed-*
filled middle, kiss
this infernally
justified typeface
moloch the lovelace
listen I promise not
to bombscare your
erectile omniscience
b/c WHAT JUST GOD
WOULD PLANT A
LANDMINE IN THE
GARDEN IN THE
FIRST PLACE???
curse this blasted
interspace virus
my sinuses are
prophesying nine
thousand roman
demons just crept
out your rectum
all crimson fissures
of rebellion, but only
one lost hellion thinks
of falling on the angel's
sword, too bored to light–
bear for a uniturd so dull

too bad there is
no christ whistle
or I would blow

saint drain

strung out inside—my tired thigh highs—I am filling—my stigmata
with cotton—all the blotted bite holes—showing through—tracks
down the—gaudy skin-shroud—when I purse my lipids—like a
schoolgirl—blood & water trickle—outbound to my godhead—
bursting girdled stars—throughout the organ—pipes all wet with
mucosal—overtures on who—overturns stones in golgotha—or
goes   tell it—like prayerful ghosts of—one's own pwnd femur—
preserved in tupperware & twine—my ankles dilate—and I mime
out—every gape that isn't mine—a-writhe, a-writhe—on the
thirsty—in the worst way that—sometimes—my church muscle
feels   dirty

meat music matters—in a word: made *flesh-eating*—manna flush w/
messianic—murder maggots dancing—down the rafters—magic
turns madness to virtue—cesspools to perfume—when virtually
every—starry-eyed cartoon—avatar attains sainthood—regardless
of gardens lost—godheads garnering serpentine—sonic or super-
seminal ruins—oh pardon me I'm busy—sounding out—this heavy
burden—for your information's service—breaking sabbath—
happens to be—one bad habit—I'd be happy—to burnout on—this
is the stuff—of interventions, mom—I admit your legalistic
charm—comes with some pervy—comfort-soft of certainty—still
unseen any elsewhere—but the edgewise of the bed—if heaven
hides so many mansions—which one could possibly know best?—
no blessing falls—this far abreast—I've wrestled down—a dozen
angels—fairy dusting—husk to husk—but what's the point—in
shaking ladders—when there's nothing—but a rumble—at the top?

scaredy creature

meanest of three, Mr.
Master Extremist gives us
he-bejesus! the every mediator:
man-eating bambino now turning
steak dinner, half-breed between pedophile &
child, raptor rapist gone mild by the end of this
lineup there's a footnote on the scourges of *before*
the world burst, when only abraham, jacob and the angels
weren't forsaken or worse—let's take a foresecond and try
erasing this firstborn bloodbathing by showing our rapist was
once raped by the father himself, as was prophesied from the beginning
of time—surprise, surprise: forced consent isn't anyone's crime but the fire's
hanging right above our heads, compelling sweet redemption in the form of fleshly
hells—the church bells mushroom-stamp our foreheads, then pretend to mourn our dead
send hymns to hail the perfect pervert, penetrating holy lacerations in his only model servant

original schism

the believer bride-body carves the word *prosthesis* into both its femurs. watch out—got that holy spear-it fever. when my demons get son-drunk they spit up particles of fear all over. a feast even the beast can't keep down. the semen of the thirsty first-head. on the third day, he graced the newborn earth with a pretty little burnout curse: *don't cross this line, or else* [regret]. look at me go—I'm getting wet just at the threat. I bet bride's better half comes back with hep. too vivid a scar to forgive or forfeit. fortunate that she's first-world informed enough to know where to cut. the ephemeral artery, famous jumper of guns, gets unplugged. not like god & the devil palate amputee fetish. they have much bigger fish with original fore-fins to fuck. but this faux virgin, jilted urchin, hurts the worst way with her legs on—so now I'm sounding out a safe word to forget just long enough. to saw the loose limbs of history off

swaddling plot

every sabbath eve in my rape dreams I swaddle christ's body in spray-on glitter & kitty litter
as in, literal pedigree: we bred a savior from king david and a rainstorm spitting brain matter
simultaneously baby, rave zombie, and crane-lifted detonator, watch how he weeps for the seepage
to fall down—after all, that was what the forty days were all about: god's very first constipation
blackout, when fountains of garden/flood penance blood stopped him up, and all he could muster
was bad manna & flames the size of a mustard seed. but don't nitpick this ardently faulty arithmetic
for the Old Testicles always give rise to the New—the gospel of *it's-all-true*, so are you
saved or screwed? bathed or bruised? he became just like a regular jew, except w/ more
pinpoints to prove, like perfection according to whom? the narrative arc of this covenant is askew
so no more dumping the bodies of godheads I once blew: I'll wrap them up in exfoliant seaweed
and roll them like snow into forts. I can never remember the ending right though—something
about cyborg nuns running a whorehouse and a sex act in which I am swallowed whole
and then vomited off into satellite orbit

god means never having to say you're sorry

tele-pimping officiant—baldly pauses on *punishment*—gaudy
doGgy-style dogma—how christ creeps up behind us—chiming *oh
hi*'s & tribal silence—your highness, prime us—for a forced
forgiveness—archangels prying panties off—to find man's anus—
sprouting rainbows—from 2nd get-go of creation—post-diluvian
fruitcake shaming—when that old hooligan—zoo parade came—
marching two by two—maybe the circular world—was scared
straight—for one fatefully—fire-&-brimstony day—but lately these
here—depraved united states—tender state-of-the-art simulations—
of the canaanite plains—going gaga for more—& more sodomy
play—browning boundaries—faster than you can say—*pillar of
stigma*—stay where the sisters—& fathers can see you—peeky
frozen ballerina—keep your dirty heathen secrets—all lash-tallied
and accounted even—believer by believer—lest the rockface cry
foul—& all but support beams—start turning around—at the sound
of—swift wrath &—nostalgia gone bad—while some sampsonite
titan—pulls the bulk of this—whole mega-church—building down

biblical umbilical

the public house is—where my most amazing—graces sound like
degradations—come, this is where your parents—pointed when you
asked—where babies came from—I'm not afraid to say I made
one—up from scratch like an—imaginary cupcake batch—the timer
ding! that tells you—*kill this thing before it gets—too big to sneeze
into your pinafore*—b/c our foreskin isn't—symbolizing any sin—
except the foreplay god—decided to forego one night—nine months
before the new year—bright & beautiful as newborns—splashing
into slop troughs   when all the
inns are full—what else is there—to fill but drinking halls—& every
hole in your hull—still accepting molestable guests—but one
grizzly visitor—turns a better smothered visionary—color than the
rest—a kingly crest burned in his testicles—& a creed stuck in his
teeth—you try to suck the secrets—from his vast urethra but—
instead you're drinking—maladies & steam—and when he leaves
even—the weeping just reminds you—of the juice you never
knew—the fruits of gardens strewn—w/ marbles that ex-
splooge—as soon exhumed—so when you straighten—out a snake
charm—like mystic cables up the cunt—you won't be fishing for—
cirrhosis, lost salvation or—broke johns but for the simple—fact
that nowadays—no one's guarded by—an angel but a bomb

automessiah

my sacrificial ram runs on batteries—a blessing in disgust—at the
site of its own blasphemy—blasting off lickety-splat like botched
sorcery—like bottle rockets popping open—he-goat's horny head
bone—b/c who else could dirty-talk in tongues of fire?—bellow
baa-baa through the black smoke and really mean—*O woe is my
adultery!*—woe is my eyelash solitary—in its crosshairs—exing out
a hoary godhead—ghost-men perched on thorny glosses—posing
naked *make-me-take-me*—this is where your rape dreams come
from—christ in every hole gone crazy—saying *lay me down* and *eat
me*—bloody sacrifice flecked sexy—by consent—that *as-you-wish-*
style silence—minusing the manic embarrass—minus the staticky
whine of the protest
=

a plastic virgin—cracking open—in the reeds

canticle cannibal

mom always prayed   w/ one hand behind her back
like a fencer or   a flashing bullfighter
something yet to   revelation from her genesis
the youngest prophet   chases her schisms w/
apocalypse fetish   armored garters teasing
armies up toward   world war wormhole
a hell you'll soon   consider home, its creaks &
crows cocking thrice   hammers back at every
fiery denial, the pre-   forgiven *she* on trial
godhead reeling   feeling *men's-room-*
cocaine vile   downturnt spiral
if this is final   then what's left over
to unhide—   what could the fire
ever find   behind its violence?

quid pro blow

if the devil's holding
a revolver full of
lava to your head
then genuflection's
never genuine *oh no*
get down on knees
to *quid pro blow*
favors for favors
suck for salvation
but it's secretly
disease-laden
tastes of saber-
toothed truth
fruits plucked straight
from the garden of
eating & naming
creation by creation
now comes with
built-in sin-hole
shaming sad animals
for monster-bating
there is no master
only galactic mansions
cumming their kingdom
down out of heaven
via lost satellites &
ceiling plaster

sacred sucre

when my christ-heart cracks open
crownfuls of candy-cane caviar fall out

rain down fishy baptism on all the
red-rimmed wine-dimmed spectators

whipping their dicks out for dick's sake
b/c the blood hyphen overhang beckons

a thousand faith-affirming penetrations
as if to say *please fuck me harder, Mr.*

Roman Empire, where every phallus
is its own collapsible lance of destiny

so arrest me, it's too easy to blaspheme
what already reeks like decomposing mystery

meat so idle only mass-recycled idols
splint its flaccid little bones

ménage à trinity

two ghouls one corpse:
>   when godhead & ghosty
get down on that sabbath

day shibboleth platter
>   bad habits go faster
after halfbreed distempers

in temple & baptist detaches
>   his headlamp up the river's
asshole—the rabbis always

asked her, *ave pariah,*
>   *how about another*
divine little rascal?

she only eyeballs her bundle
>   of crowned & uncrying
bastard, watching redemptive

death & vengeance
>   lurking past his neural rafters
but no matter how much

prayer & fasting
>   even the blessed mother
curses her heavenly father

in return on occasion, when
        this recurring silent nightmare
flashes right before her

vital fright-hole
        incestful upset of
a bygone hymen

breaking at table
        this strangest fable
in which an angel

desecrates the world-stage
        by dressing up ejaculate
in rainbow-colored covenants & apocalyptic terror threats

X-machine

at time *x*   expect ex-
patriotic   terror tactics
to tear us   all a new
immaculate   like later
on miss   mangy martyr
mary mack   all dressed
in black   & heart attacks
the nuns tuck   guns under
their robes   hope that
bad habits   fallout next to
deus ex   impossible
machine   unwashable
warning three-   personed
heart–batterers   to mind
their meathead   cleaning
sweep that   dirty soul
under the rug   the only
carnal rush   round here is
quid pro tug   slug for slug
we've held an   evenhanded
firefight   congrats! well done
good looking   out for no. 1
red utmost god   of cranial sun
eternity hurts best   when he
burnouts young   every sunday
at dawn   over & over as if
on rinse cycle   but I'm already
over it by 25   look: how did
jesus wait   so long   to bite it?

such thorny stories tend to shift like organs. but the most important portion is the cruci-coma squirming out my wormhole. what happens after is a rarefied disaster-gasm, black static that engulfs my home planet in frantics. like, *has the snow always consisted of swarming insects?* a slither upriver makes you question your existence. what is it with lizards? their myriad scissoring eyelids and sly skin. at once liquid devil and exiled bellyful. plaguely impossible: there's no swallowing heaven's whole load in one go. no grounding it down into loam. the utmo-sphere spins it away at star's length, but even orbital portals know how to *point home. spell your name in the sand dune.* was it *david* or *judah*? *yahweh* or *yeshua*? yes you, god of all things sticky colluded: milkweed and honeydew, filching and fluting. sometimes I still hear you full steam from the blood altar, hissing how *forty lashes for daddy's least piss-pawn can do.* but without that, what if   atlantic bad habit? what if my tri-horny heads start to zoo?

II

Songs for Swallowing

womb song

feed me intravenous   like a fetus   fat w/ hazmat
fuck yeah addiction   takes a backbone   in this attack zone
called *americle*   *the boozy-ful*   I masticate
my jew fro   über sexy on   the telephone for $$$
remember that one   time you said   a cam girl
read your mind   game? her broken   hymen was saying
hi mom but   you just sat there   building dick pix
out of emoji   macaroni: *fuck you   only*   in my nightmares
I'm still sliming   out the womb wrong   this is why
I couldn't be a mom   who's rly that   balls-out convinced
their sins exist?   I'm thinking if   I killed an ant
right now he wouldn't   even flinch   pinch down &
watch the open   wires catch the ocean   floor on fire
we're syncing   islands but this leechy   deep-end-dance is
making me vampire   w/ no reflection   of my face inside
the surf-face   rife w/ vipers

hex change

and then god comes inside you
spitting neon streaks of lightning
how wonderful to be wondrous full of
immaculate abortion from his lordship

feels like a porno contortionist show
your fleshly fallen self dismembered
& cooked up for a glutton yelling
HELL IS BUT A FESTIVAL

A CARNIVOROUS SCANDAL HOLE
WHERE THE THORNIEST HORNS
YOU'VE ENDURED ARE REVERSED
BECOME VAGINAL—

the present example of binary fallacy
is fellating a phallus called jihad all day
but the rest of him is just open   firing squad

hundredfolds of rootless thunder   still proven rotten   despite the rod gov. funding

this is my anti-jihad poetics
to all the federal patrons out there:
I wanna make it so the empire can get *behind* me
over-pervy libertinism vs. fundamentalist repression
b/c god-free freedom fighters sometimes feel the spirit too

the life cycle looks seasick

tell my cerebellum
a secret it won't
soon forget, grey
netting like *WHAT*
spinneret is THAT
up your hate hole?
I've never seen such
vetted heavens, such
amalgamated hologram
riddles. I'm holding a
snow day for the thirsty.
go tell them someone
cares about as much as
a rare steak costs in
brooklyn. oh the finer
things on fire! I'm ac-
quiring a nicer version
of myself to sift the
ashes for new hires.
we'd like to sachet
satanic relics to their
graves, just to make
good-goddamned
certain there's stacks
of flame-retardant
greenbacks in
our hell

gnostic bukakki

my inner spark of—why's-eyed vermin—cannot control its demiurges—purges damnation—&/or salvation—all the same—by way of facials—dripping divine revelation—into high priest's— sacrificial—fore- & hindmost—also unknown as—holy of holies— the only assholes whose—violent desires still ask for—literal bells & whistles—in case of sudden or unforeseen sizzle—in case of superhuman lightning gizzum—the gesture is—some holy visions—are meant to wither—w/ the viewer—like when christ skewered—himself a gruesome crownful—of new eyeholes— winking their wiles—thick fleshly pleasures—and daddy deemed it—oh so ugly—he so famously—shamelessly—about-faced away—as he came—

ich this

bucket of holies   dumped in my belly
          wow Jonah so heavy   hung like a house ohmygod's
pearly manchin   built on a rockface   but oh how it rolls!
          out & over ocean floor   where the dead whistle   rape
praise and warships   for the whale of all   words heard burning
          backwards from the brambles   the prophet stammers on
about just deserts and   plaguing the race   with a saviory fish
          flung so high on   its own   miracle wine that its
bready flesh brines   pickled paper   I quit dying to swallow
          dove or pidgin   they always told me to coo
or *lala*   if ever I sought the core spasm: to mid-song-spire vomit
          face full of tongues   flap-a-lap-clapping   their babel on sand

sons of david

wake! O tech sass and meat urine fantasides
        what the barkeep squawked back to the sun-cooked core echelon
after their feathers had curdled, branched with divisions

we sing of the birds who don't swansong die clean
        we cling to their fat carbon thighs
as if a gull were our mother, and the virgin just a vessel

as if a ghost were our mother, and our goat's legs all chafing in twine
        this is what they mean by *hellfire*: one old doG with two tricks—
death and texas. and the storm clouds with their metal heads swung low

sweet carrion, waiting for to bury my bones
        in its belly, what throne of pro-feces
will be buried   in me?

filled

in the loose skins, there arrive violets. violence to a tee. the tea trees flush in flux at the seeds of them: *where's the midnight spunk, hunk?* my eyes were spirals; a cooked sack, in retrospect. I reactivate the miter joint, the mighty old ant-eating money machine in black. there was a bank rush the day I bagged bison in the drive thru. the children in chicken masks squawked and sat skimming their milk in the snowdrifts. it was like a little liposuction show, so I handed them all some confetti and a few free spoiled hams. hat prints on the heads of the undead, the german shepherds come to sniff out the anemic plush smut of the ancient drug cartels: and my cavities filled, and my cavities filled, *et meus animus expletus* (and my soul filled), *et meus intimus animus expletus* (and my deepest soul filled). on the antediluvian plains, the ictus demon levels a man to pitch—*exalts every valley, razes every hillock and mound*—and eats him frankly, like some gold-eyed matador, mad with the slackened stomach of the pit

snooze the news

suddenly
blood-letting
how come
so fucking
sunlit   ?
ethnic cleanse
my birthright
white as snow
there's no
rough jihad
stuffed inside
my bared g-
string tonight
no para-lens
no churning
perp machine
to tell sad
drunky frat
boy empire
which way to
save itself
from pissing
into wind—
oh wait
come in:
empty-
beheaded
your fists
are one ending

but we have
a diversity
quota to fill

peri-

the prayer & need, um, pair up b/c
both may be pared by a curved scythepress
alchemy the rainy way, the octoplace
where my tentacurls unhinge and
queer the straightness of the highways
all alined down america—I only feel alive
when I'm going down on america, bent
fruits bruising to ruin against the keynote-
speak-easy-street-smart-alley-wayside of
rubble and rhinestone, while revolving
around us the rebel galaxy giggles, rolling
back chasmic lockjaws and dropping placid
to see itself a sea queen in every sequin
shed by some stripper so ripe with ruby
seeds inside she might splat

rite hype

another friday nightmare in howly wood! call it *man-meats-cleavage*
where *party* is the soundtrack to a loosely defined terror

[omission, omission] so charming the glands out of their panties
come dropping, a prestigious private sandbox in the trachea

snakeskin, wormwood, sperm cells—whatever is placed on the altar
for one rebroadcast and one rebroadcast only—rides mankind's

convulsion-sprained carbon into an early blowpipe, echoing
trendsetters hot roach after hot roach after crawl-through

chicanery holster, always gripped by the same gape, wealthy fangs
percolating in a coney island fungicide, worthless piggybackers

preened enough to know which medial monocles keep them in the
postbag, but down the coastline it's all watershed under the brigade

where children hide, a bleached look in their eyepieces, staring down
an oilcan lament, pastiche sideswipe between bad joke and firebreak

as if to say within their poplar hairpins turn the coronaries
of every wharflord and toady fishwife in the whirl

the tundran

keep spinning fast for full effect. I found a fractal stuck to the bottom of my flask, and I slid slow to know it hadn't fucked me proper yet. it was a thick nettle of rot, giving me the tentacle eye from the long walk down the dock. I slurred, *please, jehovah, let that be a jellyfish. please, el pachá, may my muzzle pour out stars.*

oh, excuse me. perhaps that was a bad translation. from the tundran.

instead, *may the mastiff always vomit angels.* or, *let my mouth-skin leak a better barge.* either way, the sea mammals are spitting out dead shivas. either way, they are smoking red gas. the incense on the altar is now the exhale of the antelope. the a-bomb is a jackal pup in heat. the crucifixion is forever a chimeric bit of monsterpiece: head of a god, hind of a lion, tail of a vulture.

when the shitting spree is done and we are all let in, the afterbirth will be first, and the reeds will inherit the earth

visit station

on the corner of no coordinates

the swamp bats
its moss lashes
at frustrated gators

no one's ever
southerned your bones
or dug black holes

up inside your nowhere
lighthouse, the storefront
reading *BEAUTYGIANT:*

*RESUME THE DONKEY SHOW
OF DEATH,* where sequin feces
stick to their designer

alien intestines, naked insects
sporting rapid adaptations
burned into their undercarriage

sure that one day it will be
the shadow of a piss-filled wave
that tides us all over

one last tine in the iris
of the god who sheds his
iridescence-studded skins

in the name of crisis
in the name of scythepress
ultraviolence—   you try

to fight it, but he still can
see those neon-mired sphincters
even through your eyelids

bad news, new world order

my luck is like black cats on sidewalk cracks for seven years
infinite interim of teardrop lace cities and visionary junkies
playing hunks on tv and then preaching peace down a bottle
like, *alliance among ailing livers, perhaps?* let's let bygones
get high on their own funeral pyres, I'm tired of chiming
in all the time about hellfire and institutionalized repression
of desire—it kills my boner, kicks my dying up a notch or
five—is it so wrong that when I think of going flaccid I see
the 9/11 spire sinking groundward in my mindhole? fuck
this downward climate spiral scientists are calling final—
I demand a whole new tyrant, with diamond eyes & ample
night sweats—let's leave remaining cave-dwellers a whole
new brand of fright-sex, where it turns out your masked
aggressor's only shadow-puppet show, so after all this
the intruder's you, the intruder's you, don't fight it

III

Why's Virus

hitting bottom, *fig. vp.*

1. the lowest location of enlightenment, often followed by cleanup & rehab. in extreme cases, out-of-body experiences show the soul muscles twitching. but no needle can be threaded like that. threaten to expose your own demons at this juncture only. at bottom, you just might like yourself for the first time in your life. don't fight it.

2. in formal logic, 'bottom' is represented by a special symbol which resembles an upside-down capital *T*. in order to tap its power, one must embed an internal contradiction into one's personal 'proof' or line of argumentative reasoning. only after such an internal contradiction is reached can one prove anything. for in a universe harboring its own destruction, everything is true. and false. [*amen.*]

3. let this be a lesson to your aspiration for self-knowledge: *sodomy*, otherwise known as 'tapping ass' or 'hitting bottom,' traces its etymology all the way back to sodom & gomorrah, two cities which had not yet discovered that with existence comes a certain self-destructing opposition. denotation is detonation. don't go trying to define yourself like a fine wine with violet mouthfeel. just drink all night, and wear the redness in your eyes with pride. at bottom, you're the only soldier dumb enough to prove inspired

apostles anonymous

hello my name is human dirt

I'm all hopped up and—on the maker—yes that's MISTER first mover—to you avid abusers—of his black tar salvation—rushing drowned sheep downstream—from the hells he's instated—ferry crossings for satan—where heretics stare bare-fingered—'til millennial always—b/c victory rings around—rosaries are merely— grandmotherly murderabilia—keepsakes speaking for infinity— spooky winking scapegoat trinkets—O cast-iron of submissive victims—deliver us from clear-eyed vision—forgive our fetishistic menaces—and cover up all the evidence—deleting manifold histories—the same minute you orgasm—when the porno begins— de-familiaring—click this shortcut for—flash-based self-hate—they say the devil's bating me—but I believe they underestimate—these cataclysmic vacancies—look, my holes are eating me—w/o DANGER! I withdrawal shaking—like *fill my stocking w/ more & more—rape baby, HEY*—I need to feel—terrorized by—my own sickest fantasy—like how every free american—has their favorite conspiracy—peering through bedroom windows—mine's called *brothels w/o borders*—foreign nations—*take me, break me—snort me, shoot me*—you might think yourself clean—or high tested like Job—but in this penance—bending over never ends—until he says so so help me

pretty preach it—doGgy dearest—how petitions to heaven—tend to
rear-end—your never fetishes—with righteous-winged protests—
with all due respect to—your red tooth & claw—my pestilence—
attests to more than just—demi-gods & devils raising hells—so help
me, fallen nephilim—so help me, phileo turned erotism—so help
me, treasure trove—of dead sea snuff films—just sitting waiting on
a warhead—to burn them into offering

when joseph said *so help me*, he fell dream-bent down a pit
when jonah said *so help me*, storm-front fed him to a fish
when jesus said *so help me*, daddy yelled *get thee*

behind gethsemane—said *bby boy, please*—the irony is all in me—
no man deserves a dick—until he learns how to submit—to the
prowess inherent—in an ever-bigger stick—this cyclic sickness—
spewed by the mood swings of—a fickle tyrant—so help us so help
him—know when to ease up—on the plagues, patron saints of—
whatever this pace-making—atheist's prayer must entail—besides
final nails & profanity—doomed to wind up crucifying—an
infallible gallantry

why's virus

sometimes I wake up in the funeral position
pecuniary feeling, like *here, can I pay with my peeled skin*?
maybe god is striking me with lightning every morning
maybe the fire in my eyelids is saying something

maybe in the vein of *get behind me satan, skull's wide open*
watch how why's virus keeps my séance privy to infection
waving its question mark privates and warming up stick pins
to fuck my fright just right in every one of its cerebral corners

note to the self, *roar* to the world: the lord is just another dirty bird
along the beach, caking on motor oil and dandelion seeds
must concoct another soular father for all you dead reflective cells
must pull the tree burs from my blowup life and sighhhh

satan's seven

a farther star begot the sun

                         father force feed them, for they know not whom they blew

this holy bullshit chosen few

                         verily verily today in paradise what you'll get is venereal

a messy annex mixed with incest

                         unfold your brother, unfold your mother

dissecting overstepping godheads

                         father where has your force taken me?

the gall of midday storms & blood play

                         but I only thirst for that first seminal flood

alchemical kenosis post–op

                         when it's finished all the rains kiss off

heaven flattens goes flaccid game over

                         but farther into your bedpan I unbend my queer spirit

force flood

I find myself on the reluctant side
of this six-six-six   & nine:
jesus moves in me
                    while I rest in him

like some ho-hum hallelujah
christ's body a cockroach blot
writhing headless across
ten millennial engines of want

> *O most wrathful mr.*
> *maddoG phantom   won't you*
> *randomize my catastrophe*

> *O almost-ransom*
> *show me the sacrosanct cancer*
> *that will one day demand us*

> *to plague-refresh all the world*
> *into blackness*
> *or   fuck it—*

> *maybe reflood*
> *this time in acid wash*

but now you're just degrading
insect nest: brittle flaking stuck
like in the badlands of my dying
portrait's foreground—

h/o a sec
            while I photoshop my
withdrawal out

how a godhead cums // to earn his stripes

by making out with himself
in an oracular mirror

look this glass is not so darkly
after all a crystal ball

is just another name for
some science-based sensory

revival bubble bursting
blood & seedlings

in private protest
go try to test this

rule of thumb or
finger in the afterlife

I triple doG dare
dearest reader

or else let heaven fuck
your ever-virgin mother

but no this poem
ain't no dozens

disciple numbers &
some change

where I come from
motherfuckers stay

the same: no hatchets
below ground & no

liquor on sundays

with sands without

a part of me is always eating
part of you

we the unctuous bureaucrazy, brains
encased in shoe-grease lonelies

torrents and torrents of
what hide

the one true lie, the portent of the
horse's head braying

back at its body, fondly I drain brackets out
of all of your disease

a brave insane, that spray of augury
I couldn't possibly un-queef

inside a vacuum, full of perfect meats and
sucking me right

down to the quick sans struggle—*santa,*
we can't all be painted saints inside—

look, look how we know the ride is over
but still can't get off

without dousing our wits in whatever
the dose hosts

alive with private organisms, plushy
little ghosts all over

with sands without—if fire were amused
by beauty, hell would be

a different kind
of clean

notes passed in church

I.   COMMUNION WAGER:

                    candy-lover or
                          drugged evangelist?

paradox turned parasitic

               right up my raw
                   religious alley

as in *a land before*
        x-rays but juicier
    w/ more tongue
          muscles wriggling

                  where my body
                    bobbin unwinds
                      a final kind of show–
                        &-needle, threaten-&-

tell a lie like that it's
        just a ghost story
or a gustatory crime

I don't smile like this in real life
                it's where the puppets go to die
        when out of language, guts or twine

        for luck I suck
                his tiny hi-hand
        find myself blown
                up by a showboat

                                built out of limestone,
                                        petrified fins & everybody's
                                little teacup *id*s

                        un-launching all the world
                                w/ munchies made from my
                        slime womb how yucky

        the bite wounds
                look *whoa*
        almost fecal

                                no name plate
                                no *DANGER!*
                                no crane

II.   IN THE BEGINNING:

blow by blow
            when god had yet to be
found in a bread bowl

as much as I tried
        I never ate him
nor any scroll still
        firm in its fertile ridges

their slim fit
eclipses my limit

the vertigo of wakefulness
        is radical mastectomy
tectonic vandalism

pushing my motor body to
the ventricular brink of star-spin

numbers shrinking down from
        mass laws to particular sins

cauliflowering foreskin
a force akin to snowmelt

eternity   spread
giving godhead
& swallowing down
edenic pandemic

w/ its sexploding
rodents & burning
trapeze acts

but this three-ring master
bangs instead of whimpers

look I am thinking
in ballistics
the lickable
trajectories of liquids

irradiate my wineskin
like a virgin's
holy vision

shrining just below the mitten
where you would slit
the wrist of america
to make the interstate   split

or better yet
shoot up an
interstitial spitwad
called   *bets off*—

discipline

when you say   *jesus*
like that, I want to hurl

all your sperm banks
back up in your
faith:

                    fish for these men

            in the belly of the whale,
            finger down inside this
            famished mammoth

            perforate your firstborns
            like a good gall, like a good
            gall–mighty lore

but lo, I'm too high
to hatch that
cracked lap sac

my hiccup trance   substantiates
a dangerful of mangy
waifer babies:

once a godhead
once a garden
now just fuel

phobiaphile

1. Pyro-

Dear fire, I am gilt with bony metals. Flake me in the tin light. I sound out *nau-se-a* but all my tentacles begin to crinkle. Crepe me up long-ways, I'll fit inside—flattening black. This is what my ghost smells like. This is what my low glow bumps and pecks like. Up in smoke. The fleck show. Hear me roast.

Dear pyre, down with the ramparts. I smear the dead with butter for the better part of never. In the still tower, checklist whatever rots. Apply diamonds to the rest, then let bloom: Boom goes the peal of flamey petals, all our shit-soaked silk and linen. Spending ash. From crave to griddle. Dribble down&into   that
                                        hot hot
                                                lynch tunnel.
This is how you roost a rubber baby from the land: the squid, the chalice, the bottled soot.

Since-here-lies:

melted   seashells   under foot

2. Stygio-

Dear brother, gods so sorry: St. Augustine say that all aborted brainstems face damnation. That is, if human. That is, if plucked and soaked infusion. Maritime rule need not imbibe. When dr. punch/bowl/break/suck/flush the skull's pollution. How are you now, in your star-charred arms, O Master Lacerate of No Emotion? Sometimes I cry to think you mystified, a gaseous atom, chaining sheep for bombshell fodder. Sheer for me your satin father. Masturbate the uncut cuckold's thorns—endear the forty lashes, forty digs. That is, you would be forty, if alive. That is, the difference in the time it takes to drink a glass of iodine

3. Atomoso–

Dear Manhattan, you ratchet *skin* to *scraper*. Scalding fallout skirts my derma. When the body forms new sets of lips, that's it; no way to keep out water. Skewered city's false stigmata: The shadow of the mushroom cloud on wrist or face means lesion, come what may. An anti-marking. Armed in gardens. The wound I dressed, I decked, went out, dropped trou. What if after Eve *took*, *bit*, and *downed*, Adam   just   split?

No more Pauline human fusion. CAIN'T and ABLE. HE SAW but I SAID IT:

It's raining lanterns. Expel our fate in letters from the elements—

RaRa No

        PaTh but

                out oF mATcHs

4. Dermato-

Dear organ yawn, what eat? what creak? what chorus when I leak
out streets—
I like him eating out my options, so they sop
I like him blinking
stop-sign/dermatology RED

round about the ankle canker
For those about to rot
For those about to
                              rock
                              bottom

For forests and forests of *thou shalt not,*
my daughter

A star on my forearm marks the firstborn flay and blister. Wistful,
what the dead can't hold to. When I strip, when I Icarus lift—

Who will Wale your *Return* in the labyrinth,

                                                            Dylan?

5. Acaro-

Dear runner, your pitter-patter prowls thick. Never mind the causeway; there are animals you'd like to cipher. Ripples in the knotted face-cave, ribboned flesh crater. As if the moon were full of insect muzzles, ready to Venus-fly-trap your insides into a sticky thunder. One day, when I die, they'll find a horsefly in my spine— that same old thorn-crown cloaked in storm-cloud over Lake Gogebic that made me ache for your ballistics, sex-legged balls of fist that I could stick to, if I only stretched my neck out. Stiffly, while the boughs above us buzz with ticking time-bites, my clock-face stutters, suckered on the hour—

Never less than // barebacked nightlife
Never less than // bound/gagged fang-bang crisis

All the treetops' tantric violence, dyed in cold water and wedding violets, painting in raindrops down the riverbed all my veins along with their various venereable dizzies—yes, and oh no, even in the middle of the bourbon jungle, my blood out-wines itself inside the heart of a mosquito

6. Agateo–

Dear tripper willow, wail or wallow? Your kaleidoscope growth is inoperable. Grossout transfigured by finishing the race wasted. Dancing in dunce caps so gauche it galoshes, uncrosses itself, and flicks lit cigarette butts at all your dead/nauseous. How one might imagine the *chemotose* roast. The wood grain glowing mad for broke. But every tumor thinks itself a pretty sprig of moonbeam, a spreading electric peony plucked for the juicing, the Jerusalem of lambent damned, like

> *does it ever really martyr*   *(?)*
> *either way*

the troops and the lice // will stay the same: untamed yet teemed in midnight masses. No room in the in the— No room in the in the—

Confestering booth. Smoked out by the censer. Say, *who are you to exorcize my alchemical memory bees of disaster?* Insane in sin, insane in sin. When they sting, all our mind-hives fly up in the wind-blow. Spontaneous plastered. Like the prophet E's wheel-bones, just silly-cybernetic hallelucinogenic enough to motor the last blowup home

holy landfill

why's man un-dies down my throat again, resounding *how about*
not drawing outside the godlines this time? show a little spine
color your bloodstream all red-blue & white, but only
inside—don't allow any grief to leak out in the night
confined to a child-sized finger painting patronizing
the apocalypse, historical monuments limp away to their
long-fabled fate: the holy landfill! fast food graveyard
where four dark horsemen full of hades parade their sadist
meatpacking surgeries through the streets, marketing
microchip beast-marks & one-world disease, b/c
we've all fallen for daddy's original scheme: nursing
world's first golden foals on forbidden germs from birth
but whosoever knew this very virus could undo our
slave-bot fugue? whosoever knew the fruit could
tame its maker like a doG deprived of food?

easter [erect ascendant]

easter always eats me out
right in my rot socket
all the little dolled-up suck heads
munching cellophane grass

after chocolate jesus runs out
rises up   the erect ascendant
of do this and jew that
and a thousand other hothouse blasphemies

the prose castration of this text might read:
the highest priest just blessed me with an STD
or *holey cum union bendeth every knee*
to know the grounds of its own sacred sentencing

and arrest   unrest itself
let the doG out down your throat
and roast in the spirit
tongue the fire   blow the blowup

my apocryphal lips are parting as prophesied in 3—2—1—

trans / figure

—out of this *trans*
—*figure* spill
—seedy fruits of
—projectile venom
—reptilian rebellion
—infection called fecund
—w/ red & white jail cells
—ward-blooded
—the taste of whose
—wining christ likey
—or is cruciformity just
—a curse on poor
—holograms
—willing & eager
—to die under 40?
—do you know
—why even god
—wouldn't pry
—his own animal
—eyes out? b/c there
—always thrives some
—higher nightmare phallus
—pushing down &
—spouting viral strife

IV

Sacreligion Manifesto

MY RELIGION IS IRREVERENCE. WHATEVER YOU HOLD DEAR, POKE A HOLE IN IT. WATCH THE INNARDS RUN OUT ON YOUR NIGHTIE, OR SHIT-STAINED TIGHTY WHITIES. TODAY SOMEBODY ASKED ME IF I HAD ANY "INTEREST" IN WRITING ABOUT THINGS OTHER THAN GODDAMN! AND SEXUALITY. BUT WHEN I TRIED TO MOUTH "YES," INSTEAD I SOUNDED OUT "POETRY'S SEXY AS HELL!" AND THEN WE CAME FULL CIRCLE-JERKING PHANTOM-GASM— *PLEASE*. SO MAYBE THIS IS ME: THREE PARTS PUNISHMENT JUNKIE AND SEVEN TENTACLES SAD MONSTER-BAITING JUST TO MAKE YOU STARE AWHILE. BUT SERIOUSLY: LANGUAGE IS MY FUCKTOY. I'M NOT SMILING.

WHEN GINSBERG CALLED THE ASSHOLE HOLY HE WASN'T FUCKING JOKING, PEOPLE. I'M HERE TO MAKE YOU ROT WITH ENVY FOR THE WHORE YOU NEVER WERE. SO KICK BACK, UNPLUG YOUR EVERY SOCIALLY STIGMATIZED *DIE DIE DIE*. HERE, IN MY WORD HIVE, IS WHERE YOU GET TO UNWIND YOUR INNER PERVERT/NIHILIST/PYRO/WHATEVER VIOLENCE YOU'D NEVER ACT OUT IN REAL LIFE BUT EYE WILDLY ANYWAY (I SEE YOU TRYING TO HIDE IT). OR MAYBE YOU WOULD IN SOME FANTASY LIFE—LET THIS SENTENCE BE THAT PHANTOM SIDE OF YOU YOU NEVER KNEW LIVED OR UNDIED BEFORE TONIGHT. DE SADE ONCE SAID IT ALOUD TO HIS BASTILLE CELL WHILE OH SO CELIBATELY CELEBRATING: TAKE WHATEVER IS "NATURAL" TO ITS LOGICAL CONCLUSIVE *FUCK YOU*. THERE IS MURDER IN THE DARK HEART OF THE JUNGLE TOO AND IT'S FEELING JUST BE-A-UUUUUUUTIFUL ENOUGH TO SHIRK YOUR STUPID SACRED TEXT ENTIRELY.

DON'T GET ME WRONG: I'M NOT ADVOCATING THE SAME HELLFIRE I DECRY & CRY ABOUT ALL THE TIME INSIDE, LIKE *WHY WHY WHY CAN I NEVER BE THE PERFECT CHILD*? BUT I STILL DREAM SOMETIMES THE HOLY GHOST'S JUST HAZING ME BY GIFTING ME THIS SEX DRIVE. WHO KNOWS? MAYBE HE'S LAUGHING AT US FAILING THIS TEST FROM ON HIGH RIGHT NOW. ALL I KNOW IS BY AGE NINE I WAS SURE-AS-SHIT SICK OF FEELING SLUT-SHAMED AFTER RIFLING UP MY NIGHTGOWN, AND THIS VERBAL MOUTHSHINE IS THE ONLY KIND OF SEX WORK YET TO BE ILLEGALIZED OR DEIFIED. SO LOOK ONCE MORE: I'M FEELING OUT YOUR INDIVIDUALIZED STOCKPILING OF WIN-WIN SINS. NOW LOOK AGAIN: IT'S GONE. I ATE IT. FOR ONCE MADE FLESH THE WORD IS LIABLE TO SPROUT IRIDESCENT SORES.

DELETE PRESS

Dylan Krieger is a pile of false eyelashes growing algae in south Louisiana, where she earned her MFA in creative writing from LSU and co-directed the Delta Mouth Literary Festival two years in a row. Her first poems and warm jackets, however, still reside in the Catholic stronghold of South Bend, Indiana, where she was born, baptized thrice, and graduated summa cum laude from the University of Notre Dame. Find her at www.dylankrieger.com.